Limit of Liability/Disclaimer of Warranty

While the publisher and author have used their best efforts in preparation of this book, they make no representations or warranties regarding the accuracy or completeness of the contents of this book. The publisher and author specifically disclaim any implied warranties of merchantability or fitness for a particular purpose, and make no guarantees whatsoever that you will achieve any particular result. Any case studies presented herein do not necessarily represent what you should expect to achieve, since business success depends on a number of factors. We believe all case studies and results presented herein are true and accurate, but we have not audited the results. Fictional situations are used to distill various aspects of tradeshow marketing and management to more easily demonstrate situations that can and often arise in real life situations. All fictional characters are clearly identified. The advice and strategies in this book may not be suitable for your situation, and you should consult your own advisors as appropriate. The publisher and the author shall not be held liable for any loss of profit or other commercial damage, including but not limited to special incidental, consequential, or other damages. The fact that an organization or website is referred to in this work does not mean that the publisher or author endorses the information the organization or website may provide or the recommendation it may make. Further, readers shoud be aware that Internet websites listed in this work may have changed or disappeared after this work was written.

Copyright © 2019 Mel White and Classic Exhibits Inc.
All rights reserved. No part of this book shall be reproduced, stored in a retrieval system, or transmitted by any means, electronic, mechanical, recording, or otherwise, without written permission from the publisher. Although every precaution has been taken, the publisher and author assume no responsibilty for errors or omissions. Nor is any liability assumed for damages resulting from the use of the information contained herein.

ISBN 978-1-709454-01-1

For more information, please contact:

mel@classicexhibits.com
linkedin/in/melmwhite
twitter.com/melmwhite

503-652-2100
www.classicexhibits.com

Design & Illustration — Meredith Lagerman

What's So Funny About Trade Shows?

Table of Contents

4	Introduction
5	Why Every Trade Show is Like a First Date
7	What Zombies Can Teach Us About Trade Show Marketing
10	Dumb Stuff People Do at Trade Shows
13	7 Questions You'll Never Ask About Your Trade Show Display
17	Why Are Marketers So Bad at Trade Show Marketing?
21	10 Common Myths About Trade Shows
26	Trade Show Tips From Sasquatch
30	What Not to Wear
33	Has Your Trade Show Booth Expired?
35	Fast Food to Fancy – Restaurants and Trade Show Exhibits
39	Is Your Exhibit a Nilla Wafer, a Fig Newton, or an Oreo?
43	Your Trade Show Booth Staff Kinda Sucks
45	The 40 Things You Do at Trade Shows That You Would Never Do Anywhere Else
49	Trade Shows in Westeros – Game of Thrones Characters as Exhibitors
53	20 Clues Your Exhibit Has Expired

Introduction

If I Didn't Laugh, I Would Cry

We've all experienced those moments, when as the saying goes, "If I didn't laugh, I would cry." I can't think of a better expression to describe trade shows. For most marketing professionals, trade shows represent one of their biggest challenges. They typically have limited experience with designing an exhibit or planning for the show. And the written (and unwritten) rules can be opaque and frustrating. Far too often, marketers waste a lot of money before they understand how to be successful at a trade show.

This guide is intended to supercharge your knowledge about trade show marketing whether you are a novice or a trade show warrior. And to do it as painlessly as possible.

Feel free to jump around. There's no linear beginning or end.

Finally, a big thanks to all the readers who proofread this book and gave me advice. Your contributions were invaluable.

Enjoy!

Mel White, VP of Marketing and Business Development
Classic Exhibits Inc.

Why every Trade Show is like a First Date

Trade shows are like first dates, first meetings, or job interviews. These "firsts" scare us. They should. No matter how well you prepare, the unknowns trump the knowns by a ratio of about 10,000 to 1. If you've ever been on a blind date, or even a first date with someone you've just met, you know that a date is **about being the person you strive to be**, not the person you are.

Of course, not everyone has the gumption, the imagination, or the self-awareness to lift their game to the next level. **Some people never grasp that first impressions are lasting impressions.** They wear scuffed shoes to the job interview, slouch in the chair, chew gum, or dress inappropriately. They make the decision easy for the interviewer. On that important first date, when every word and every gesture is scrutinized, they monopolize the conversation, talk with their mouth full of food, and tell jokes that would offend Andrew Dice Clay.

I suspect, however, that **most of us strive to make a positive first impression**. After all, we want to be liked, and we want to be respected. In a typical social situation, we engage others in conversation in order to learn about their lives and to share ours.

Looking Bad

Let's start with the booth. Too often it's a bulletin board of artwork stuck to a booth. Or, if it's a professionally designed exhibit, it's long in the tooth, damaged, and the exhibit equivalent of Archie's jalopy, sitting on cinder blocks. **It screams, "I just don't care."** You may be comfortable with a piece of kale stuck in your front teeth, but even if your date has matching green dental jewelry, chances are there will not be a second date. Trade shows are expensive, but the actual display is usually the least expensive investment over 2-3 years. **Invest wisely.**

Behaving Badly

Rather than riff on the stereotypical cell phone-chatting, hungover, couldn't give a rat's @$$ booth staffers, let's take the high road. The reason too many exhibits are staffed with the wrong people is simple: They are the **wrong people**. They don't have a vested interest in the company's success, they aren't knowledgeable, and they aren't 'people' people.

Trade shows are not magazine ads or television spots. They are **face-to-face sales opportunities**. How often have you been to a Chamber of Commerce mixer and the local bank's display is staffed by a teller? The teller is pleasant, but he/she doesn't know anything about the bank's loan programs, CD rates, or charitable guidelines. The teller shouldn't be there. The local branch manager should be. Pamphlets, key chains, and a bright smile are not replacements for one-on-one knowledge.

Ideally, your **trade show staffing should have senior management participation**. They have the knowledge and the vested interest. Too often, however, they wander the show floor like a band of middle-school bullies whispering snide comments about competitors, eating candy, and planning the evening's activites. Never underestimate the power of a title. And unless your senior management is poison, meeting the CEO or President of a company can turn "interest" into an "order" almost immediately.

> **Never underestimate the power of a title.**

> Want to succeed at your next trade show? Treat it like a first date. Look your best and mind your manners. Remember that first impressions are lasting impressions. And no matter how tempting that kale omelet looks for breakfast, it's probably a good idea to select the oatmeal instead. ;-

What Zombies Can Teach Us About Trade Show Marketing

Trade Shows and the Undead

Surprisingly, trade shows and zombies have a lot in common. Sometimes in a good way. Who would have thought that zombies could be a role model for your sales and marketing team?

Single-minded Focus

Appearance Matters

Teamwork

Lights, Motion, Noise

You may not appreciate their all-consuming desire to eat your flesh, but they are committed to the task. They let nothing get in their way, except an axe to the brain.

Your next trade show will be wildly successful if you make it a priority.

You never forget your first impressions of a zombie: filthy clothing, greasy/unkempt hair, and rancid halitosis. It's sad but true — we judge people by their appearance.

Your company spent considerable money to participate, so shine your shoes, press your shirt, and dry-clean that blazer.

Zombies travel in packs. That teamwork ensures them a much higher percentage of kills. There's a reason "We Killed It" signifies success.

By working together, those poor, doe-eyed attendees don't stand a chance.

The undead and the living are both attracted to lights, motion, and noise.

When planning your booth, ask yourself "Will my exhibit attract 200% more zombies than my competitors?" If the answer is "No," you need to get creative (or consider a ceremonial human sacrifice every day).

What's So Funny About Trade Shows?

Intelligence

Zombies love brains and so should you. Being smart about your trade show marketing means you understand that trade shows are not the same as print ads, videos, brochures, or traditional sales calls.

Trade shows are opportunities to attract new customers and strengthen existing relationships.

Fresh Meat

Ever notice that zombies won't eat other zombies? They like their meals fresh.

Fresh ideas and innovation, particularly during a weak economy, propel one company forward while leaving another one struggling to survive.

Trade show attendees go for two reasons: to find solutions to existing problems and/or discover innovations that will strengthen their operations or bottom line.

Know Your Customer

In zombie-speak, good customers freak out and get eaten. Bad customers ram a metal rod through a zombie's skull. You want good customers, just without the "getting eaten" part.

Good customers become good customers because we understand them and tailor our product or service to meet their needs.

Preparation Matters

Zombies don't need a trade show toolkit, an exhibitors handbook, or an exhibit designer. They are 100% prepared the moment they go from living to undead. You're not so lucky.

You won't succeed without thorough pre-show, show, and post-show preparation.

Without Customers, What's the Point?

Wandering aimlessly is pointless, even to a mindless zombie. Zombies crave excitement. When a living, breathing human enters its proximity, a zombie switches from listless to high alert. Serious exhibitors react similarly, albeit without the growling and moaning.

If the attendee is interrupting your game of Angry Birds (and that annoys you), then you need to re-think your priorities.

There's No Cure

Once a zombie, always a zombie. **If you love trade shows and are serious about trade show marketing, there's no antidote.**

It's in your blood. No matter how hard you fight it, once bitten, it's incurable.

DUMB STUFF
People Do at Trade Shows
It's Crazy! And So Easy to Fix.

People do really dumb stuff at trade shows — consistently dumb stuff. Anyone who participates in trade shows could write a book on what they've seen. Pre-show marketing and post-show leads alone would cover several hundred pages. Let's concentrate on the quick, easy fixes — the ones you can change before your next show.

Senior Management

Clients want to talk to senior management. Bring them...but not *all* of them. Bring the President and the CEO (assuming they are personable and knowledgeable). Don't bring them if they love to hear themselves talk. Don't bring the CFO, the COO, or anyone who couldn't charm a goldfish into a fishbowl. Their presence demonstrates that your company is serious about the show. **In today's business-centric world, the CEO and President are rock stars to your audience.** This rule obviously doesn't apply if you do 80 shows a year. Pick 3 or 4 of the most crucial and have the "chiefs" there.
Tip: **It's much easier to get a trade show marketing budget approved if senior management participates.**

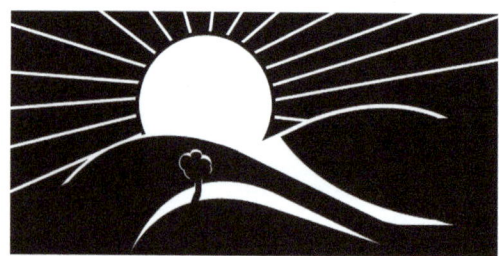

Come Late, Leave Early

Most shows allow you to enter the show hall early in the morning. This gives you time to organize the booth and make any last-minute changes. More importantly, it's **the ideal time to walk the show, see industry trends, and get a better sense of what your competitors are showing**.

If possible, bring a colleague; that way you can compare notes. It's also a great time to talk to the other early birds. There are fewer distractions, and you're more likely to have casual and informative conversations. Staying late has similar advantages. *Tip:* Not surprisingly, **tired exhibitors can be very revealing at the end of the day.** That said...adhere to the formal and informal rules of the trade show floor. Don't do anything you wouldn't want a competitor to do in your booth.

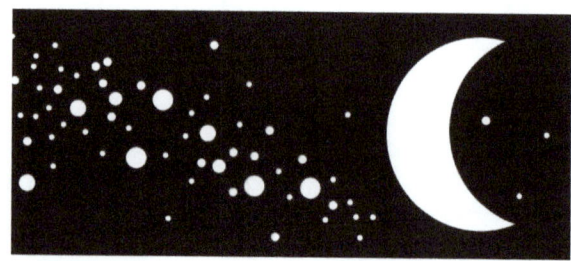

10 What's So Funny About Trade Shows?

Ignore the Competition

Many companies are arrogant about their competitors. They see themselves as "the leaders," so what could they possibly learn? The answer is — a lot. Even knowing that you are the leader is valuable when targeting new markets and developing your marketing strategy. Unless your company prohibits it, don't be afraid to introduce yourself. Friendliness is not a crime. You may be surprised at what you'll discover — a friendly competitor has been known to send business your direction if the client doesn't fit their model.

Tip: Sometimes competitors can be sneaky smart about their sales, trends, and products. What they share may be a red herring intended to mislead.

Ignore Your Customers

It happens. It's human nature. We feel like we don't have to spend as much time with existing customers since we know them. However, your customers come to trade shows to learn about new products, meet new people, and share challenges. **They want to feel valued.**

If a good customer says "I was at the show, but —

    a) You were so busy no one was available
    b) I was there but just never made it to your booth
    c) I spoke to Bob and he said there's nothing new happening"

—then you have a problem. A *correctable* problem, but a problem nonetheless. Prepare for their visit. It can be as simple as a pre-show email that lists the topics you would like to review in the booth.

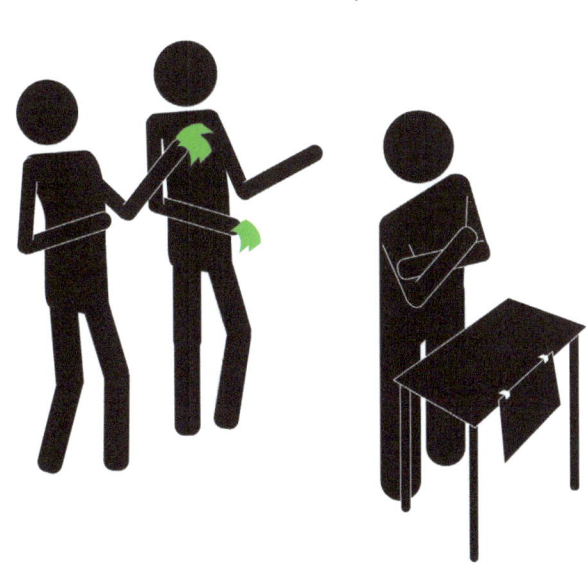

Ignore the Social Events

As much as we want to pretend otherwise, trade shows are business in a semi-social setting. The planned social events, such as the evening gala, meet-and-greet events, award ceremonies, and receptions are still business functions. Make it worthwhile. It's your chance to meet new people, chat with industry colleagues, bond with existing customers, and find new customers.

Can it be hard, especially if you're a wallflower? Yes... but wallflowers have an advantage. They are great listeners and in any large room, the ratio of talkers to listeners is about 95:1. Ask the right question (or sometimes *any* question), and the rest of the night is on auto-pilot.

Tip: **For anyone under 30, Social Media is an effective tool with potential customers, but you still have to talk to people. You can't just text them.**

Rely on Memory

Unless you're Sheldon from *The Big Bang Theory,* your memory is hopelessly flawed. On day 1, you will recall every single conversation. By day 3, an important client will remind you that you spoke for 30 minutes about a critical new project on day 1.

Use whatever works — paper, tablet, business cards with notes, digital recorder, etc. Yes, it's better if everyone in the booth uses a similar system, but it's even better if everyone takes notes that can be reconstructed at the end of the day, or at the end of the show.

Tip: **Don't let "Joe" leave the booth at the end of the day without emptying his pockets. Otherwise, those notes and business cards will be trash can casualties or unreadable smudges by next week. Collect and save them. They are as valuable as gold.**

7 Questions You'll Never Ask About Your Trade Show Display

There's no substitute for experience

It's time to buy a trade show display. Unlike lawn mowers, cameras, or smartphones, there's no Consumer Reports. You do your research on the web, and if you are smart, you consult with a trade show exhibit professional. You ask the right questions about design, assembly, and how much it weighs. You even ask to see the warranty.

However, there are questions you won't ask. How do I know? Because no exhibit manager has ever asked me these questions... and they should!

1. Will the Display Look the Same After 10 Shows?

Have you ever bought a screwdriver at a discount store only to have the tip bend? You throw it away and realize that a Kraftsman isn't a Craftsman.

About 60-70% of all trade show exhibits have a skeleton of aluminum extrusion. Sometimes it's visible, sometimes it's not. **The dirty little secret is that it's cheaper to use low quality extrusions with thin walls and a sub-par finish.** Over time, it distorts, mars, and looks tarnished. Your new booth becomes a used booth before you've wrapped-up your current marketing campaign. Quality extrusions have thicker engineered walls and use higher quality metal.

Ask about the manufacturer of the extrusion. There are recognized names and then there are Kraftsman. You may not recognize the name but that's the beauty of Google. If someone tells you, "an extrusion is an extrusion," walk away.

2. What's the Quality of the Fabric Graphics?

The rise of "fast fashion" has revolutionized the apparel industry. There's a market for disposable fashion. It's cheap and attractive, but the fabric is thin and the sizing inconsistent. But no one expects it to last or have the attention to detail of high-quality apparel.

Fabric for graphics, like clothing, is not all the same. **Most inexpensive displays are shrouded with thin, stretchy fabric made with low quality zippers or cheap velcro.** And yes, there's a pecking order to hook and loop as well. The cheap fabric graphics are meant to be disposable… even if it's not sold that way. You can feel the difference. Trust your hand.

You can feel the difference. Trust your hand.

3. What's the Quality of the Fabric Printing?

No one ever thinks about this. But they should. Dye-sublimated printing, the predominant type of printing for fabric graphics, is a high-tech process. As with any technology, **the latest and greatest is old news in about 12-18 months.** The previous generation of dye-sub printers get sold to second or third-tier printers. If you've ever seen the difference between an HD dye-sub graphic and a 4-color one, you know what I mean. Skin tones are more realistic. Black is black not dark grey or navy blue. There's no color banding . You get the picture.

Ask when was the printer was manufactured (not re-manufactured or purchased). Even if it's only been owned by a little old lady in Pasadena and stored in a garage, it's still an AMC Gremlin.

14   What's So Funny About Trade Shows?

4. Is the Packaging Material Reusable?

You just bought a new pair of Beats by Dre headphones. They sound great, but you decide you want them in black and not fushia. Good luck getting it back in the packaging. It was meant for marketing, not for re-marketing. Far too many trade show displays are packed to prevent damage before the first show. But what about damage after the second, third, or thirty-third show?

High-quality reusable packaging costs more than bubble wrap and thin foam. **Smart, well-engineered packaging is like finding $20 in your dress pants. It's an unexpected miracle that keeps on giving show after show.**

> **What about damage after the second, third or thirty-third show?**

5. Are Replacement Parts Available?

Folks send me photos asking me to identify a part. That's rarely an issue if it's from a major display manufacturer. However, it's usually from a $699 pop-up or tube structure. Let's be honest. There are no parts. There never were any parts. It wasn't sold to have replacement parts any more than a $17 toaster. It's meant to go into the landfill after a half-a-dozen uses.

Now if that idea appalls you, then **ask your supplier if quality replacement parts are available, what is the cost, and how quickly can you get them.** If they are only available through Smiling Sammy's Display Store, that's a really, really bad omen. He's gotta a guy who knows a guy. Good luck with that.

6. How Do You Handle Wire Management?

There's no middle ground on this. **It looks good or it looks really, really bad.** Those electrical and A/V cords have to go somewhere. More often than not, the cord management for most exhibits resembles a hairball. But it doesn't have to be that way.

You have to share what electrical devices will be in the booth and where they'll be located. Your supplier needs to know this, including anything electrical you are renting. Ask your supplier about their solution for lights, monitor cords, etc. If they stumble — run. It means the solution is likely to resemble white twist ties from trash bags.

Ask your supplier about their solution. If they stumble – RUN.

7. What are the Designer's (Exhibit and Graphic) Qualifications?

Everyone is creative. Up to a point -- chainsaw sculptures, toilet roll cozies, saw blade paintings. I'm not here to judge. Well, maybe a little.

Most of us are out of our element when it comes to exhibit and graphic design. And like wire management, there's no middle ground. **Great exhibit designers have years and years of experience working on a variety of projects** (custom, portable, modular) with collaborative input from other exhibit designers. That's how they get experience, perspective, and context.

The same is true with **graphic designers** but with a twist. They **must have experience designing graphics for trade show displays**. That's the key. It doesn't matter if they are rock stars with web design or print advertisements. You don't want an occasional trade show designer to be the lead designer. If you have an in-house designer familiar with your brand, then make the design process collaborative. Graphic design for trade show displays is a craft. Trade show designers have learned what works and what doesn't to attract attendees on the show floor.

These questions may make your trade show exhibit supplier uncomfortable. Good. That's how you'll know if you chose the right one.

Why are Marketers So Bad at Trade Show Marketing?

Some marketers will hint at it. Others will grumble. Then there are the ones who are honest. They don't understand trade show marketing. That's not surprising.

It's rarely taught on the undergraduate or graduate level. At best, it's mentioned in passing in a textbook. I know. After earning an MBA, I went to work for an exhibit builder. On Day 1, I was clueless. I'd love to say that trade show marketing is marketing, but that's not entirely true. It's specialized and more unpredictable than other forms of marketing. And, depending on the company, it can be more difficult to measure results.

3D vs. 2D

Marketing has traditionally been 2D: print and television, brochures, websites, etc. It's also been static and somewhat controllable. Trade show marketing or face-to-face marketing is as much about human interaction as the message or the branding. **It's about creating conversations, before, during, and after the show.**

Trade show marketing is as much about human interaction as the branding.

Then there's the booth design. That's outside most marketers' comfort zone and the dollars involved make it even scarier. It's easy to panic when the costs begin to hit six digits for even a modest island exhibit.

What's So Funny About Trade Shows?

Variable Measurements

Unlike print, television, or web ads, there are no standards or reliable source for subscriptions, ratings, or clicks. Counting leads works, but it's a crude measurement. More sophisticated exhibitors track pre-show promotions, leads, and sales through the entire sales channel, but they are the exception.

Competitors

Trade shows are truly a competitive sport when it comes to marketing. It's the one time you and your competitors are all in the same room, all vying for the attention of the same audience. You see what they're doing… and vice versa.

Uncontrollable Variables

No one likes unpredictability when it comes to their marketing campaign and implementation. Despite one's best efforts, trade shows can be chaotic. Freight doesn't arrive on time. Items are broken. Flights are cancelled. An exhibitor on the far side of the exhibit hall is giving away beer and sandwiches. The exhibitor nearest you has their music so loud you can't talk to potential clients without shouting.

Unfamiliarity/Knowledge

Most medium-sized companies participate in 2-5 trade shows per year. Some as few as one. That makes it challenging to become an expert quickly. In addition, each show has a different audience, different rules, layouts, and resources. Too often, when the internal "expert" understands how to maximize the company's trade show efforts, that person is assigned to other responsibilities. Then someone new has to start fresh.

Sales and Marketing

Before, during, and after a trade show, sales and marketing must be partners in the dance. You're a team. **Face-to-face marketing requires sales skills and marketing expertise perfectly choreographed.** And no matter how much sales and marketing claim to play nice, there's always a wall at most companies. It's that wall that dooms most exhibitors from fully benefiting from their trade show program.

How To Become An Expert:

1. **Go to trade shows as often as possible as an attendee.** Ask questions and listen to what works and what doesn't. Plus, be willing to take classes at industry events about trade show marketing, even if your goal isn't to become a trade show certified manager.

2. **Rely on your local trade show professional.** If they only know how to sell a display, not how to succeed at trade show marketing, then find someone else.

3. **Tap into industry consultants.** These folks know how to avoid the potholes and the meandering paths so often taken by trade show exhibitors. You can find them on LinkedIn, Google, or by simply asking your local vendor.

4. **Plan to succeed.** Create a comprehensive plan that targets pre-show, show, and post-show marketing and put specific goals in place for each one.

10 Common Myths About Trade Shows

1. Trade Show Marketing is Marketing

If you're a skilled marketer, you will grasp the nuances of trade show marketing, but it will take time. Most marketing managers gravitate to their strengths by focusing on the structure, the graphics, or the show promotion and planning. Intellectually, they know these are interconnected, but they may not know how to maximize their results.

Work with professionals, whether it's a graphic designer, an exhibit consultant, or a certified trade show manager. Trade show exhibit marketing is a craft learned the hard way through trial and error. It's easy to burn through a lot of money before you figure out what works and what doesn't. Don't stumble through a year or two of mistakes when exhibit experts can save you time, money, and embarrassment.

2. Trade Show Labor is Hostile, Incompetent, and Expensive

No one will dispute that trade show I&D can be expensive, particularly in certain well-known venues. However, **most I&D contractors are very competent. They can solve almost any last minute trade show display crisis.** You may disagree with the show hall rules regarding labor regulations, but the actual laborers in your booth didn't write them. If you disagree with the rules, don't take it out on the person assembling your display. Contact your I&D labor provider or show management.

You have the power to control your labor costs, beginning with exhibit design. Consider assembly and packaging during the design phase. Are the components labeled, can it be packed without relying on a 20 page manual, and are the packaging materials reusable?

3. Trade Shows are One Big Party

For some companies, that is true. They wine and dine customers to excess, party until daylight, and don't attend any show sponsored events. Inevitably, those are the same companies that grumble about their trade show ROI. They spent "X" but can only measure "Y" sales from the show.

When you ask them about their pre-show promotions, their lead qualification, their client meetings at the show, and their follow up with prospective customers, **you get a big "Huh?" They didn't plan their trade show marketing program, and now it shows.**

What's So Funny About Trade Shows?

4. Anyone Can Staff a Booth

Too often, companies send the wrong folks to work the trade show booth. Even worse: they don't train them. **Not everyone has the temperament, the knowledge, or the discipline for a trade show.** Here's my rule: **Find those employees with previous retail sales experience who love assisting customers with product or service solutions.** It doesn't matter if they are in Sales, Marketing, Engineering, or Production. **What matters is their attitude and their knowledge.**

Want to know who not to send? "Joe." Every company has a "Joe." He drinks too much, he gambles too much, and he wanders around too much. About a half a dozen times a day, you'll wonder what happened to Joe. Five minutes ago he was sucking down his third espresso, leaning on the counter, and engaging in a Twitter war with a YouTube influencer. Suddenly he's gone . . . AGAIN!

5. Trade Shows are a Waste of Time

If you love sitting in a cubicle creating spreadsheets, then, yes, a trade show may not make sense to you. It requires you fly to desirable locations like Las Vegas, San Francisco, Orlando, New York, New Orleans, or Chicago. You have to meet people, listen to their needs, talk about your company, stand on your feet, and generally be helpful, pleasant, and knowledgeable. Even worse, you may have to join clients for breakfast, socialize with them after show hours, mingle with potential suppliers, and attend educational seminars about your industry. That's really tough.

You either embrace the opportunity to build sales and learn something new, or you grumble about the airport, the food, the hotel, and the hassle of time away from the office. **It's all about your attitude.**

6. Trade Shows are Expensive (Part 1)

True, as is almost any investment in capital equipment or advertising. Let's explore this from another perspective. Say your company purchased an $18,000 inline display (10 x 20). Let's assume your company participates in 4 trade shows a year and you expect the booth to last 5 years. Take the average cost per show including show space, literature, airfare, hotels, meals, entertainment, transportation, and labor. If you are frugal, you'll spend:

> **$25,000 PER SHOW**
> Multiply that by 20 shows (4 shows x 5 years) = $500,000
> Divide the booth cost $18,000 by the $500,000 in expenses
> = 4.3% — this represents the display cost to total expenses

Let's take it to the next step. Your company takes trade show marketing seriously (and you should). You conduct pre-show promotions, send the right folks to the show, and aggressively follow up on all leads.

> **On average, you demand $150,000 in new sales from each show.**
> $150,000 x 20 shows = $3,000,000 in sales.
>
> Based on those numbers:
> $500,000/$3,000,000 = 16% return on show expenses
> $18,000/$3,000,000 = 0.6% display cost to sales

I don't know about you, but those numbers look pretty good to me. Unlike magazine, television, or direct mail advertising, they're measurable if you put the right metrics in place.

What's So Funny About Trade Shows?

7. Trade Shows are Expensive (Part 2)

Probably 60% of all trade show displays never go to large industry shows in Las Vegas, Orlando, or Chicago. The owners take them to Chamber of Commerce mixers, local business shows, corporate events, regional industry shows, and hiring and recruitment fairs. At these shows, you won't see island exhibits, but you will see pop ups, table tops, banner stands, and lightweight hybrids.

These displays range in price from under $200 for a basic banner stand with graphics to $8000 for an upscale portable hybrid. **Considering the cost of most advertising, buying a trade show display is a bargain by comparison and one that you'll use for years.**

8. All Shows are the Same

If your experience has been that "all shows are the same," you may be approaching every show EXACTLY the SAME. Not every show has the same audience. There may be similarities, but the attendees vary, even in shows focusing on the same industry.

If you are serious about trade show marketing, then **contact show management and request attendee and exhibitor data.** Have them describe the goals, mission, and audience of the show. Then go to the next step, and ask for exhibitors who have been loyal to that trade show for many years. Assuming they are not competitors, contact the Marketing Manager or Trade Show Coordinator. **Ask them why they attend, how they tailor their message to the audience, and how that message differs from other shows.**

Then do what professional marketers do: create a message, design appropriate graphics, and plan a pre-show, show, and post-show campaign.

9. Trade Show Leads are a Waste of Time

Leads can be a waste of time if:
- You collect business cards in a fishbowl for a cool product giveaway like an iPad
- You don't qualify the attendees who visit your booth (or jot down their needs), and
- You don't contact them until a month or two after the show.

More than anything else you do at a trade show, **your lead quality is a byproduct of your pre-show planning, booth staff training, and timely post-show follow-up.** There is a direct correlation. A trade show is a salesperson's nirvana, namely a captive audience that spent money to see you.

You may get lucky and acquire a game-changing customer while sipping coffee, clipping your fingernails, and chatting with co-workers, but that's rare. **Finding good customers takes time, enthusiasm, knowledge, and patience.** You have to be at your best because they can (and will) walk down the aisle and find another solution.

10. Virtual Trade Shows will Replace Real Trade Shows

There is a place for virtual trade shows just as there is a place for dating websites. But at some point, you have to meet in person. And unless you're looking for a mail order spouse, you're not going to get any action unless you shake hands, look one another in the eye, and share your story face-to-face.

> *...your lead quality is a byproduct of your pre-show planning, booth staff training, and timely post-show follow-up.*

Trade Show Tips From SASQUATCH

Sasquatch is no 7 ft. dummy. He/She has a brain to match that brawn. Bigfoot understands marketing, knows PR like a Madison Avenue insider, and can out-Kardashian the Kardashians without taking a step outside the Pacific Northwest. Here's what our "ancestral brother from another mother" can teach us about trade show marketing.

It's Possible To Be BIG and Still Not Be Seen

All too often, exhibitors are told that an island exhibit will get them more leads, more traffic, and more attention. **A poorly executed island with bland graphics and a confusing floor plan is much worse than a well-designed inline.**

Mystery Has Its Allure

Bigfoot knows the benefits of the tease. Revealing teaser information, before the show, about a new product or service creates anticipation from customers and the press. Apple is a master of this technique. So is Bigfoot. **Being coy with a well-crafted marketing campaign before the show has its benefits.**

Tap Into Your Followers

You won't see Sasquatch sending press releases or tweeting. His followers do all the work. They have websites, Facebook pages, and a television show that keeps our big, hairy friend in the news. Occasionally, a rogue "fan" will damage the Bigfoot brand with a silly stunt, but that's an acceptable risk with any loosely organized group. Even then, the realfollowers rally around the brand and repair any damage.

Spend Your Marketing Money Wisely

Technically, Bigfoot doesn't spend any money, at least that we know of. But that doesn't prevent him from getting maximum exposure. He's got a TV show (Finding Bigfoot) and a website (www.bfro.net). **Your trade show marketing doesn't have to be expensive. Planning is crucial.** For example, team up with other exhibitors on a prize that would be too expensive for one company, but not for 5 or 6. Then create a theme or event that gives everyone more foot traffic and exposure.

Training

After all these years, why hasn't Sasquatch been captured? Training. There are no unprepared Bigfoots. They know how to respond to nearly every situation, whether it's a sudden encounter with Boy Scouts or a deer hunter. **Exhibitors who "arrive" at their booth without adequate training will fail.** Unfortunately, it's the most controllable part of any trade show marketing program, and most exhibitors simply "wing it."

Leave Your Mark

What's the point of participating in a trade show if you don't leave your mark? Bigfoot routinely leaves the big three: foot prints, hair, and scat. It shows he's been there and people take notice. No one is advising you to leave the "big three" at your next show, but **making a lasting impression is critical to your company's success.** Is your message clear? Does it show how your company can solve a potential client's problem? How do you engage the attendees in the booth? And finally, are you following up on leads after the show?

Smells That Linger

Bigfoot sightings often include a description of an unpleasantly acrid or skunky odor. That's not good, but no one expects our tall friend to bathe with Irish Spring. You, on the other hand, should do the following:

▸ Clean that sport coat or blazer once in a while. Just because it doesn't look dirty doesn't mean it doesn't reek of B.O., Subway $5 foot-longs, and Vegas casinos.

▸ Coffee breath. No one's telling you not to have a Dunkin' in the morning. Drink away, but for goodness sake, don't assume your breath will smell like rose petals after 5 cups. *Tip:* **Breath mints are every exhibitor's best friend. Take several.**

▸ Perfume and cologne. We aren't living in 17th century France, masking bad hygiene and a fear of bathing with strong fragrances. If you insist on smelling like a celebrity, a little goes a long way.

The Brand is Important

You already know this, but occasionally, marketing managers think they can treat branding at a trade show the same as branding in a magazine ad. **3D marketing has a unique set of challenges which only advice or experience can teach you.** Rely on your local trade show professional to guide you. You'll save money, time, and headaches. There's a reason the Loch Ness Monster is no longer in the news: poor branding. That's not a mistake Sasquatch ever plans to make.

Rely on your local trade show professional to guide you. You'll save money, time, and headaches.

FAMILY

How often do you hear of Bigfoot sightings where the dad, mom, and kids are frolicking in a stream? Never. Being Bigfoot is serious work and families can be a distraction. No one is telling you not to bring your family to the industry trade show.

If you are serious about maximizing your trade show investment, you already know that trade shows are not a vacation. Not only are you on your feet at the show all day, but there's also meetings before and after the show with suppliers, clients, and coworkers. There's the pressure of responding to emails and calls while away from the office. And nearly every show has non-stop educational and social events.

Learn From the Big Guy and Maximize your Trade Show Marketing Potential

What NOT to Wear

Are You Really Wearing That?

I'm no fashion expert. The yellow sweater I wear all winter is a dead giveaway. But you don't have to be a member of the fashion police to spot these faux pas. Wear what you want if you're an attendee, but as an exhibitor, consider these suggestions.

Shoes

Rule #1 You want to look your best, so you buy new shoes. Who hasn't made this mistake? They look great, but by 2 pm on Day 1, all you can think about is how much your feet are throbbing in pain. By Day 3, your blisters have blisters.

Rule #2 There's a balance between attractive and professional and casual and comfortable. Find that balance. Even if you have carpet and padding in your booth, you are probably not used to standing for hours and walking on concrete floors.

Rule #3 – Take a little initiative and shine those puppies. Or at least get them shined at the airport while you're waiting for your plane. It's cheap even with a generous tip.

Rule #4 – The belt is supposed to match the shoes guys! A brown belt with black shoes? Your mother would be appalled. Socks should match too.

Slacks, Dresses, Blouses, and Skirts

We all pretend we haven't gained weight. But we have. Don't wait until 7 am on the first day of the show to discover your clothing doesn't fit. Unless I missed something important in Biology class, blood flow is important. Buttons and zippers are amazingly strong, but even they will eventually cry "Uncle!" -- often at the most inappropriate times.

Tip: If you feel the need to make "discrete" adjustments more than twice a day, you are probably wearing the wrong size.

Clothing

Rule #1 Anything you would wear to the beach, yoga class, house painting, hunting, jogging, fishing, or a play date with your toddler on a rainy day in the park is probably inappropriate. Obviously, there are exceptions, depending on your business model. However, professional does not mean formal. Dress like you are the distant relatives of the wedding couple, not the couple themselves. In general, it's a good rule to dress at least one step above the trade show attendees.

Rule #2 Here's the easy way to decide on logo corporate apparel. If it looks great at a college basketball game, it looks silly at a trade show. I don't care if it's the latest high-tech, super-duper sweat-wicking material. There's nothing wrong with corporate apparel. Most companies will have their employees in shirts, sweaters, blouses, etc with the company logo but there's a right way and a wrong way to do it. Tasteful, subtle, and clever will attract more attention than garish.

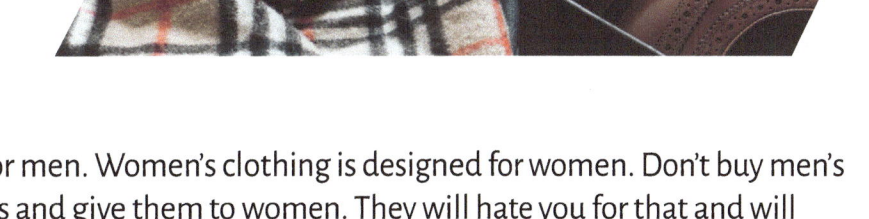

Rule #3 When you shop for corporate apparel, resist the urge to go cheap. I know. You are only wearing it for three days so why pay more? Because cheap clothing looks cheap and it looks even cheaper when embroidered. Plus, you want your staff to be comfortable and confident. Nothing undermines that more than ill-fitting, tight, bagging, or translucent clothing.

Rule #4 Men's clothing is designed for men. Women's clothing is designed for women. Don't buy men's polo shirts, t-shirts, sweaters, and vests and give them to women. They will hate you for that and will refuse to wear it. I know. I made that mistake and am still hearing about it.

There are exceptions to every rule, but in general, just remember there's a reason why Fortune 500 executives don't wear golf shirts and skinny jeans to negotiate multi-million-dollar deals.

Perfume/Cologne/Scents

Do you remember the dirt cloud that surrounded Pigpen in the Peanuts cartoon? We all know people who douse themselves in a scent cloud. Scents should be alluring or soothing. They are less effective when they elicit migraines or seizures in others.
Tip: Some advice on how much to apply – use *one* free sample from the magazine.

Jewelry

Wear want you want. There are no rules, just a word of caution. **Expensive, heirloom, or bulky jewelry may not be the best choice.** Trade shows are all about handshakes, hugs, and distractions, all in an unfamiliar location where jewelry can get lost, damaged, or stolen.

Pockets

Finally, whether male or female, pockets are a must. As an exhibitor, you need pockets for business cards, pens, trinkets, breath mints, etc. I'm not talking about a safari jacket with 37 pockets, but wearing a jacket, slacks or skirt with pockets will make your life much easier in the booth.

What did we miss? We'd love to hear your "What Not to Wear" suggestions and comments.

Trade show displays, like yogurt and milk, have expiration dates. While it may not be printed on the box, it's not hard to spot one that's starting to spoil. Here are 20 Clues that it's time to buy a new exhibit.

1. Graphics are attached with Velcro to a fabric backwall. While that may be OK for a FFA display at the county fair, it's no longer acceptable at a professional trade show.

2. I&D won't touch your property without hazardous duty pay. When show labor has to don hazmat suits before starting an install, that's not a good sign.

3. Duct tape is an important design element. And you're excited it now comes in designer colors – Baja Blue and Desert Sunrise Yellow.

4. When your booth was purchased, a quarter could transform your hotel bed into Vibrating Magic Fingers. AaaAAaaHHhhHHhhHHhhHH.

5. Attendees compliment the "vintage" theme of your booth and graphics. "Very retro!"

6. You decide to re-print your graphics and hand the graphic designer a floppy disk.

7. There are more "just in case" parts than actual display parts.

8. The shipping labels have added 50 pounds to the weight.

9. You lust over the two $99 banner stands in the adjacent booth.

10. The 'No-Questions-Asked, Lifetime Warranty' has expired.

11. It smells like the Pennsylvania Convention Center. Even Febreze can't kill that odor.

12. You found your distributor by flipping through the Yellow Pages.

13. Your storage costs have exceeded your purchase price by a factor of 10.

14. Your graphics have a "Happy Days" theme, and The Fonz is still your unofficial spokesperson. Ayyyy!

15. Someone tagged your crate with the Rolling Stones tongue graphic (and you think that's cool).

16. It folds, and weighs more than an AMC Pacer.

17. Children flee in terror as if they've seen a circus clown.

18. Your competitors gush over your booth – "Don't change a thing! Seriously. Not a single thing."

19. You found a "Win a Free Palm Pilot" Promotion Flyer in the case.

20. Your boss says "By golly, it was good enough for Old Joe, God rest his soul."

If you recognized any of these, put your display in the recycling bin.

Fast Food to Fancy
Restaurants and Trade Show Exhibits

What Do Trade Show Displays and Restaurants Have in Common?

Many inexperienced exhibitors struggle with their display options. And who can blame them? Even for hardcore marketing professionals, trade show exhibits can be puzzling and the prices bewildering. Some displays are hundreds of dollars, while larger projects easily climb into six figures.

How do you choose? Oddly enough, **trade show displays are a lot like restaurants**. Yes, restaurants. There are fast food displays and fine dining exhibits. Don't want fast food or fine dining? How about casual dining displays? Where you eat depends on your budget, your taste preferences, and your priorities. Let's take a moment to compare the familiar (restaurants) with the unfamiliar (trade show exhibits).

Fast Food

A fast-food restaurant provides the quickest food and service at the cheapest prices. The decor is simple, and the selection limited. Going to Taco Bell, KFC, and, of course, McDonald's is almost always convenient, predictable, and inexpensive, but not always healthy.

Finding fast food displays is just as easy and convenient. There's no shortage of imported banner stands or tension fabric displays on the web, all available with just a click or two. These displays serve a purpose for local events or for small businesses not participating in professional trade shows. **They are cost-effective graphic mediums with limited accessories and an uncertain lifespan.** Just like a burger, fries, and a Coke, they taste great but should be consumed in moderation. The experience is nearly always transactional, not consultative.

Fast Casual

Unlike fast food restaurants, fast casual restaurants are more likely to serve healthier choices and offer more comfortable dining rooms. Customers usually order their food at the counter, although drive-thru and takeout is available. Think Chipotle, Boston Market, or even Panda Express. And while you have choices, those choices don't include cooking the Kung Pao Chicken, for example, without chicken or peanuts.

Fast Casual Displays are typically purchased from a local exhibit professional, although they can be ordered online. **These displays offer more accessory options such as shelves, monitor mounts, lightboxes, etc.** There's usually a conversation or consultation between the buyer and seller about their specific product or marketing needs. **The packaging is better. The quality is better. And while they are often based on pre-configured "kits," those kits can be re-configured within limits.**

What's So Funny About Trade Shows?

Casual Dining

Casual dining restaurants offer a wider menu selection, table service, and a family-friendly environment. Servers offer advice, take orders, and serve food. The prices are higher than at fast casual, but are more affordable than fine dining restaurants. Chains like Applebee's or Cheesecake Factory are casual dining, as are locally-owned restuarants.

Most corporate exhibitors who participate in industry-specific trade shows fit into this category. They work with local or regional exhibit designers/builders to design a system solution or a customized exhibit. As exhibitors, they want **an exhibit that reinforces their brand, presents a professional appearance, and adapts to their trade show marketing program without breaking their budget.** More often than not, they are receptive to custom rental solutions if the design offers more flexibility and visual impact, but at a cost lower than purchasing an exhibit. They appreciate selection, value, and service, and they welcome guidance from a knowledgeable exhibit marketing professional. The experience is almost always consultative.

These exhibitors appreciate selection, value, service, and welcome guidance from a knowledgeable exhibit marketing professional.

Fine Dining

Fine dining restaurants come with the most elaborate menus and expensive prices. Owners of fine-dining restaurants want to present an atmosphere of elegance and grace. They employ chefs who attended culinary schools and possess many years of experience.

Fine Dining exhibits, like fine dining restaurants, **are equal parts atmosphere, presentation, quality, and experience.** They are almost always memorable, and their size and creativity can be a magnet for attendees throughout the show hall. Most are pure custom, both in design and construction, although subtle and effective modular construction has become more common. These exhibits are more likely to include LED Video Walls or AR.

Larger island exhibits or double-deck structures are most like fine dining, but inlines (like 10 x 20 or larger) can project the same elegance and upscale appearance. It's possible to achieve this level of sophistication without spending hundreds of thousands of dollars, but it requires the right exhibit partner and a commitment to all facets of trade show marketing (and not just the display). A steady diet of fine dining, just like one of fast food, is rarely healthy or cost-effective for most exhibitors.

It's possible to achieve this level of sophistication without spending hundreds of thousands of dollars.

Hungry for successful trade show results? **It all starts with choosing the right display** for your marketing goals and budget, as well as working with an exhibit professional committed to your long-term success. And yes, we all love french fries and chocolate milkshakes, but a more balanced diet is always a better choice.

Is Your Exhibit a Nilla Wafer, a Fig Newton, or an Oreo?

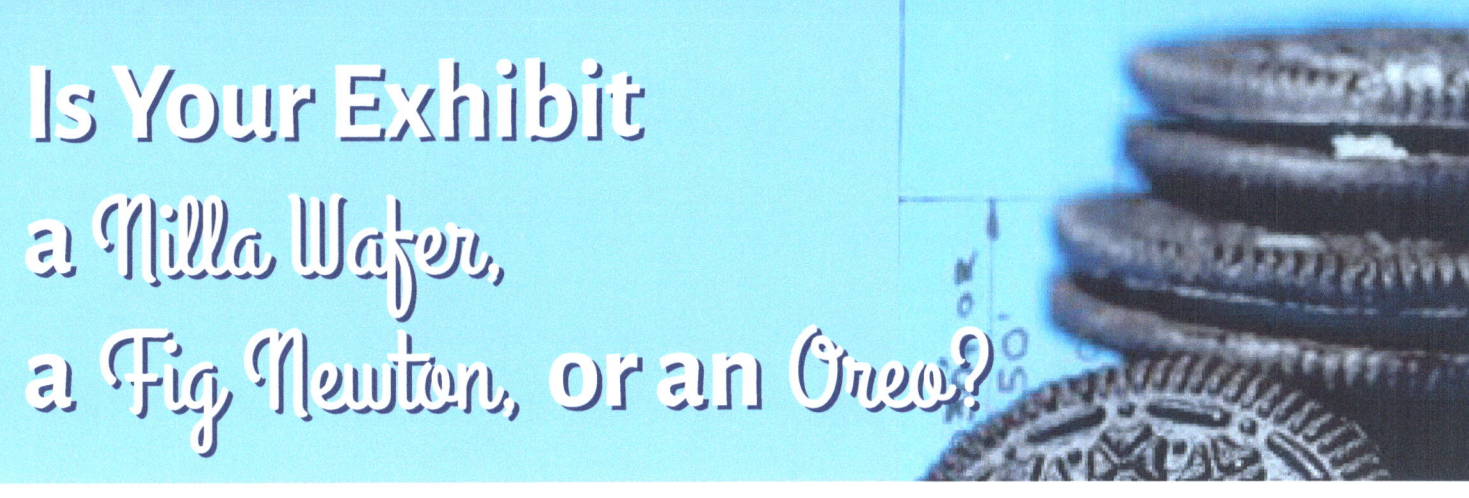

Sugar and More Sugar

As someone who grew up in the 60's and 70's, I consumed a lot of sugar. I mean A LOT. Kool-Aid, popsicles, Shasta pop, ice cream, breakfast cereal, and every Hostess snack from Twinkies to Ding Dongs (perhaps the best product name ever!).

My parents would gladly eat sugar wafers or ginger snaps. Not us kids. **We fought for Oreos. Would settle (but not be excited) for Fig Newtons. And pouted if given a Nilla vanilla wafer** (unless drenched in banana pudding). This experience gave me a solid foundation for judging things. **As an adult I can rate just about everything on a cookie scale.** I'll limit myself to Oreos, Fig Newtons and Nilla wafers, but be assured that the "science" behind my methodology includes frosted animal cookies, Pepperidge Farms (as a collective group), Girl Scout Thin Mints, and Chips Ahoy.

When it comes to trade show exhibits, there are pop-ups, hybrids, modular laminate, custom, and basic tube and pillowcase graphic displays. But those are just labels, and not practical, oh-so-satisfying cookie evaluations.

What's So Funny About Trade Shows?

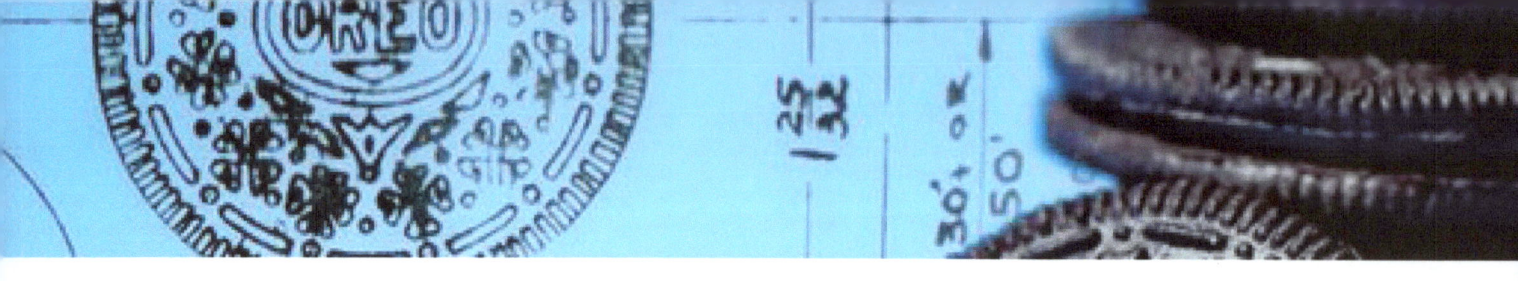

Nilla Wafer Displays

If you notice these inlines, it's usually for all the wrong reasons — fuzzy graphics, broken hardware, or a general "vanilla" appearance. In addition, they're bland in design and accessories. No monitor, shelves, pedestals, storage, or charging stations. No tablet stand, computer, or lightbox. It's a tradeshow display in the same way a Nilla wafer is a cookie. Basic, unassuming, aesthetically similar to every other opening price point display. **It got you there, but no one's going to assume you're a Fortune 1000 company.**

Fig Newton Displays

You either love Fig Newtons or you don't. There's no in-between. The equivalent inline has the same characterisitcs. Attendees are drawn to it because it takes design risks. There may be curves, headers, accessories, and a creative counter with storage. The graphics are layered with a mix of fabric and direct prints. **Fig Newton displays often come in a variety of "visual flavors," each with slightly different creative variation.** You'll never mistake a Fig Newton display for a Nilla Wafer one. And while you may not always like everything about it, attendees notice it on the show floor, which is what exhibitors want.

> **Attendees are drawn to it because it takes design risks.**

40   What's So Funny About Trade Shows

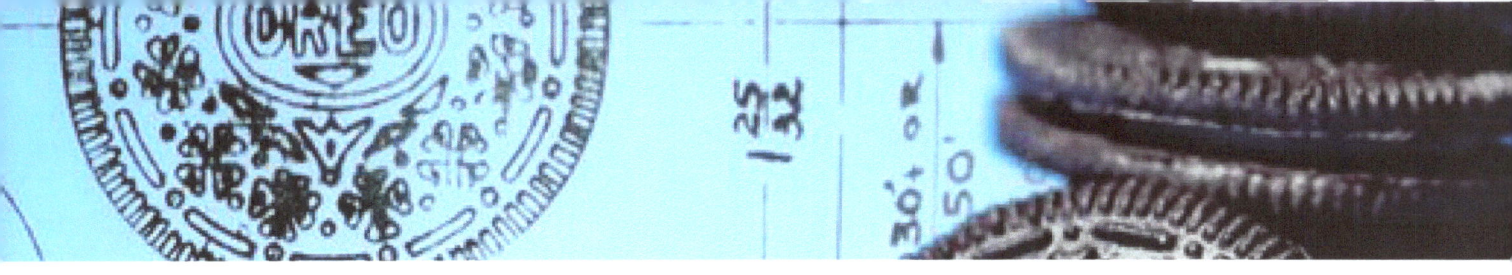

Oreo Displays

Oreos are the cookie equivalent of royalty. The traditional Oreo is the king; there are also Oreo queens, dukes, counts, princesses, and barons. They rule in a 20th century sort of way. No real power, just a commanding presence that demands respect.

You've seen these 10 and 20 ft inlines on the show floor. The booth is beautiful. The graphics are spectacular. The design, the aesthetics, and the function are seamless.

The booth is beautiful. The graphics are spectacular. The design, aesthetics, and function are seamless.

You approach it, mesmerized by its allure. You find yourself lingering. Need water? It's there. A freshly-baked treat? They have a tray of brownies. The product video is captivating. The lead retrieval questions never seem threatening or intrusive. **You understand what they do, and yet, you still want to know more.** It's not that the exhibit is expensive. It's that the design is flawless, and the booth staff is attentive, knowledgeable, and professional. **It's that perfect display "cookie" which always satisfies and can be tailored to your trade show tastes.**

What's So Funny About Trade Shows?

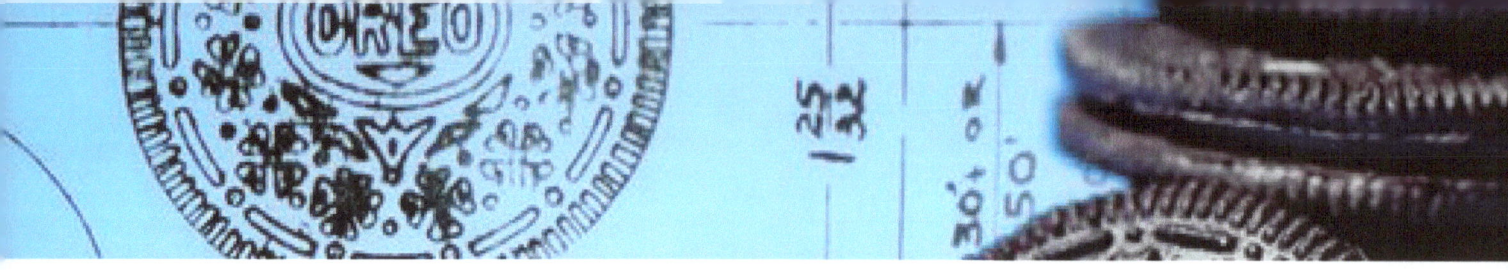

You have a choice in inline displays, just as you do with cookies. But unlike cookies, when it comes to a trade show display, you are not choosing what you want but what others want. How do you want to attract attendees? How do you want to be perceived? And lest you think it's all about price, it's not.

Well-designed inline displays come in all price points. And well-trained booth staffers are priceless. If that seems intimidating or overwhelming, never fear.

Find an exhibit house with an established history of success and grab onto their coattails. They understand trade show displays, and possibly cookies.

> **When it comes to a trade show display, you are not choosing what you want but what others want.**

YOUR TRADE SHOW BOOTH STAFF Kinda SUCKS

This shouldn't surprise you. **You know your staff needs help.** They are lazy. They don't know the products. They look like hell after Day 1. And, worst of all, they don't have a clue why they're there. Yet, you tolerate it show after show. Why? There shouldn't be any reason why your staff isn't spectacular. **It's time to put on your adult pants and do it right.**

WHO SHOULD BE THERE

That's easy. **Bring employees who know the products or services, have charismatic people skills, are personally invested in results, and participate in pre-show planning or post-show implementation.**

Two out of four doesn't cut it. A trade show isn't a vacation. It's a strategic investment. You'll often hear that 80% of trade show leads are wasted. Personally, I don't trust that statistic, but I do know that bringing the right employees to the show solves that problem. They won't let a lead sit on someone's desk or be forgotten on a jump drive. They're relentless about post-show follow-up because they understand how much time, effort, and money went into planning and participating in the trade show.

> **A trade show isn't a vacation. It's a strategic investment.**

WHAT DO THEY KNOW

What they know is important, but what they do with that knowledge is critical. **You want the Information Dream Team in your booth.** Whatever the question, there's someone there who has an answer, or can find someone who knows the answer.

Just knowing stuff isn't enough. Each staffer must capture every sweet, savory nugget of information the attendee shares. Everyone thinks they'll remember that game-changing conversation from Day 1, but by Day 3, they couldn't tell you their own spouse's middle name even if you gave them the first three letters.

Just knowing stuff isn't enough.

Trade shows are exhausting physically and mentally. There is zero chance you'll remember the details even if you have an eidetic memory. Honestly, the lead retrieval system doesn't matter. **What matters is having a system that your group understands and follows.** You can't be a namby-pamby about this. There should be consequences for not following the information capture process.

BOOT CAMP MENTALITY

Trade shows are a battlefield with winners and losers. On that battlefield, strategy and implementation trumps raw brute strength every time. What are the goals? Is everyone clear about them? At a minimum, **there should be a strategy and planning "booth camp" meeting before the show.** Then, there should be alignment meetings every day before the show opens. Some companies even have meetings after the show hall closes to review leads, answer questions, and prepare for the next day.

More than anything, **you have to be flexible.** What you thought would be the "go-to" product or service at the show may take a backseat based on attendee feedback. Then there's going to be a wild card. Often, it's an evolutionary or transformational new product or service introduced by a competitor. At that point, you have to decide if your show strategy changes.

TOUGH LOVE

In any pack, there are always the stragglers, the injured, and the just plain stupid. You can ignore them and allow them to be food for your competitors, or you can deal with the problem. The staffer who arrives late sweating tequila and lime, reeking of three cups of espresso, better have a good reason, like entertaining your key client until 4 am. Same with Susie Smartphone or Standing-on-the-Sidelines Sam. This isn't a soccer tournament for 8-year-olds where everyone gets participation ribbons. It's a competition where sales, money, and jobs are on the line. **Everyone has to pull their share.** At tough love companies, the Susies and the Sams get sent home via Greyhound with loose change for vending machine sandwiches.

When it comes to trade show staffs, you get what you tolerate. When you expect more, your team will rise to the challenge. Set clear expectations, communicate your goals, plan your strategy, and manage the environment, the days, and your post-show communication. It's not easy, but your team (and your boss) will sing your praises when it's "Go Time!"

> **When you expect more, your team will rise to the challenge.**

The 40 things You Do At Trade Shows

you would never do anywhere else!

What might seem normal to the trade show community is often viewed as bizarre to those who rarely set foot in a trade show hall. Below are 40 Things You Do At Trade Shows You Would Never Do Anywhere Else. Enjoy!

Throw trash in the aisle and expect someone else to clean it up

Spend $8.50 for a 12oz bottle of Aquafina

Pay someone to look the other way… and brag about it later

Max-out your credit card on one transaction (drayage, perhaps?)

Wear matching unisex clothing

Grab anything worth less than $10 (candy, hats, pens, mugs…) to take home

Share steamy industry gossip with competitors

Chat with 500 total strangers

Gush about the double-padded carpet in booth #1108

Buy a gaudy belt from the casino gift shop for $165 after forgetting to pack one

Party until 3 am with Steve in Accounting, Larry in HR, Melissa in Engineering, and Rebecca in Quality Control

Bum breath mints from strangers

13. Arrive at work at 11 am. Leave at 3 pm

14. Get agitated when someone walks across the corner of your booth space

15. Take a Lyft to Lowe's at 9 am for last minute supplies

16. Pretend you don't smell that awful, face-melting smell

17. Debate the existential meaning of portable, modular and custom exhibits

18. Act interested in (insert topic)

19. Complain about how much it costs to vacuum 400 sq. ft. of carpet. Vow to do something about it

20. Allow strangers to take your stuff for 3 days and not know where it is, how it's being stored, or if it will be returned undamaged – and with zero ability to get it back early

21. Let someone point a lead scanning device or smartphone camera in the general vicinity of your chest and crotch. Repeatedly

22. Be convinced a 15-minute conversation will lead to $500,000 in new business

23. Assemble a 3D structure that costs somewhere between a new car and a McMansion, only to disassemble it 3 days later

24. Spend 20% of your annual marketing budget over 5 days. Never calculate the ROI, vow to do something about it

25. Compare the work ethic in Philadelphia, Boston, NYC, Chicago, Orlando, Anaheim, San Francisco and Las Vegas to that of your hometown. Vow to do something about it

26. While you shower, hang your clothing in the bathroom to steam out the wrinkles

27. Explain, once again, to your family and friends that it's a "business trip," not a vacation

28. Get visibly excited by the phrase "traffic congestion"

29. Guard your giveaways like a momma bear on Day 1. Beg show labor to take them in bulk on Day 3

30. Sneak off to the bathroom for a quiet place to work

31. Hide in a storage closet to scarf down a scone, while dusting your co-workers coats, purses, and briefcases with gooey crumbs

32. Judge people based solely on their name badge

33. Convince your boss that 300 fishbowl leads are new clients clamoring for your product and not the iPad giveaway

34. Pretend the son of the company president is not still drunk. Allow him to talk to potential clients and competitors

35. Spend 3 days with 100 of your best friends and not speak to them again for 362 days

36. Fly from the Midwest in January to Las Vegas, Orlando, or New Orleans and NEVER leave the hotel/convention center complex

37. Reintroduce yourself to the same person three times.

38. Toss the sales literature you carefully collected over 3 days so there's more room for tschotskes. Pretend they're for your kids

39. Be really, REALLY EXCITED to leave Las Vegas or Orlando

40. Finally... wonder (after scanning the room and mumbling quietly to yourself) why the Federal Government hasn't filed RICO charges against certain segments of the trade show industry. Vow to do something about it.

Trade Shows in Westeros
Game of Thrones Characters as Exhibitors

Yeah yeah, you've had enough Game of Thrones analogies, articles, and opinions about how the show ended. Me, too. I get it. But, bear with me for just ONE MORE because I bet you haven't read something that compares your favorite characters with – you guessed it – Trade Show Exhibitors! So, sit back and contemplate who you are, or rather, who you want to be and see if this makes sense — unlike the ending to GoT.

Arya

Arya exhibitors are underestimated but won't stand for anyone's bull. They work hard and hone their skills slowly and wisely, making a list and checking it over and over. Arya exhibitors reach out to learn from the masters. **They take notes, practice until their skills are formidable**, and plan for victory each step of the way.

They surprise their adversaries and show up fearless to every show and walk away triumphant. But don't be fooled; they aren't perfect. **They learn from failures.** Step-by-step they keep getting better, and more clever, and eventually shatter their competition like a total boss.

Sam

OK, so these exhibitors might not always be the front-runner "winners," but you have to love them. They might be a little timid at first and need some hand-holding but, dang, are they loyal. They trust those they deem experts (like their exhibit house professional), and they are generally open to new ideas and strategies.

However, these exhibitors are not pushovers: they are intelligent and perceptive, so **don't perceive their willingness to follow as a weakness**. Their intuition is spot on, and in the end, their steady strategy pays off consistently. They also tend to befriend the right people and create meaningful and lasting professional partnerships on and off the trade show floor.

Tyrion

This "wanna be" 50 x50 exhibitor excels in a 10×10 footprint. They are smart and clever, making the best of what they are given. **Strategy is their king, and they make wise trade show marketing decisions in the beginning, winning the trust of many big clients.** But then, over time, their confidence (and a few bad habits) gets the best of them, which leads to more foolish choices as they grow.

They aren't *evil*, just overly confident in their own abilities. But don't worry, the Tyrion exhibitor is ultimately a strategic player and will wise up and get it together by partnering with the right supportive team. Eventually they will GROW into a brilliant 20×20 booth. Still not the biggest, but it's perfect for their awakened goals.

Sansa

Sansa exhibitors are supremely confident, intelligent, skeptical, and bold. They exhibit with a honed strategy based on learning from past failures (traumas). They are "under the radar" triumphant and have their own loyal following, who will be forever faithful.

Clients stick with them for the long haul, and their activity in the booth is mostly current customers looking for "what's new" from their favorite vendor. Oh, and they have a design aesthetic that cannot be beat... their booth will always look stunning.

JON SNOW

Essentially, an outcast who really isn't. Have you ever seen an exhibitor who shows up and their booth looks a little boring on the surface, but darn it if their booth isn't the most popular? **They are cautious, slow and steady but they listen and make real connections with their booth visitors and loyal clients.** They make bold decisions when necessary but know how to read the room. They choose their shows (battles) wisely and strategize with a team to ultimately create a winning plan.

They are humble to a fault and never see all that they could be, allowing others to shine more brightly on the show floor and in business. But they don't go broke (or dead), so their ROI is impressive. They may decide to partner with a front-runner, trusting that's the right thing to do and hoping for mutual success. When it's proven to them that they are actually better (their clients tell them so), they refuse to believe until they must make the ultimate sacrifice... choosing themselves to WIN (maybe they steal that larger booth space from their partner... gasp!). But it's OK: their fans are supportive and loyal.

DAENERYS

Imagine these exhibitors were start-up companies but with the help of a few huge investors, they grew BIG, fast. **They began with nothing and were perceived as weak and easily taken advantage of.** But then, (born out of fire) they shoot out into the industry with the biggest dragon of them all -- MONEY. They spare no expense, and they have it all: formidable assets (killer booth and amazing swag) and an army of booth staff in matching shirts.

They are coming for a fight with the confidence to win. And they do win, until they break. Emotions get the best of their strategy and something bad happens. Can they recover? Hmmm?

What's So Funny About Trade Shows?

CERSEI AND JAIME Cersei exhibitors think they are ruling the show floor and take no help or compromise from anyone. Other exhibitors sense their arrogance and are out to attack and overcome this misguided leader. Their "twin," maybe a sister-company (ok, brother, but that's not the colloquial term), is along for the ride and follows the lead. **This sibling company may have a wandering eye seeing what others do and their success, but ultimately stays loyal to their leader, for better or for worse.**

This talented hero is known by all the land, but all of a sudden, that fame is taken swiftly and #thestruggleisreal. Jaime exhibitors once had it all: fame, fortune and literally the world in both of their hands (ha ha), but when they least expected it, someone took their most valuable asset (maybe their biggest client?) and now they feel lost. Loyalties realign, and a new beginning is on the horizon, but **old habits (and endings) die hard**.

I could go on and on, but with over 150 main characters in Game of Thrones, we'd be here literally until Winter. On that note: Ready for one last GoT cliché? **Winter is Coming. And in the #TradeShowLife, Winter is the TIMELINE.**

Your show is coming and planning ahead is the only way to defeat the White Walkers = RUSH FEES. Knowing this... I think GoT got at least one thing right. #AryaStark

ERICA DOUGHERTY, EXHIBITS NORTHWEST
erica@exhibitsnw.com

20 Clues
Your Exhibit Has Expired

1. Your last legal source for halogen lights is now a frozen yogurt store. Your next option is a dark web site run by a dude with the handle "NotWearingPants."

2. Your 19" flat screen monitor was made by Zenith.

3. Six months ago, you bought a display from a company that specializes in imprinted coffee mugs and keychains. Surprise, surprise. The display lasted for one show.

4. EXHIBITOR Magazine includes your exhibit in its recent article, "A History of Portable Displays from 1995."

5. Your repair kit is a shoebox with zip ties, Velcro, duct tape, a box cutter, Tylenol, a hammer, lipstick, and fifty mousepads.

6. There's a COMDEX label on your crate.

7. Your logo hasn't been that color since the Bush administration. The FIRST one.

8. Jimmy, your labor guy at Moscone, remembers setting up your booth at TS2. Whenever he wants your attention, he says, "Hey, Whippersnapper!"

9. Two (very painful) words: Foldable Truss.

10. You put your glasses on only to discover that your graphics are even fuzzier.

What's So Funny About Trade Shows?

11. "Parts and pieces" means something different now than when the display was new.

12. You think SEG stands for "Some Extra Gravy." It makes you very happy when anyone asks if you want SEG.

13. Your graphics are printed on a vinyl banner and have grommets.

14. Show organizers keep suggesting space near the restrooms because of "all the extra traffic you'll see."

15. You play *Eye of the Tiger* in the booth and your hanging sign announces you are "Risin' Up to the Challenge of Our Rival."

16. Your exhibit house stores your crates near the fire escape. They've stenciled a skull and crossbones on all four sides.

17. The manufacturer had to entice Eddie the Machinist out of retirement with three bottles of Jack Daniels to fulfill your order for replacement parts.

18. The storage closet smells like Becky's perfume, and she quit 11 years ago.

19. Your portable display case has more stickers than the VW van of a Grateful Dead groupie.

20. Your colleagues are always busy whenever you ask for volunteers for a January trade show in Las Vegas or Orlando. And your company is based in Fargo.

Bonus:

When You Bought Your Display...

- You were addicted to TAB.

- You paid a bribe to get your kid a Teddy Ruxpin.

- Your new car came equipped with ashtrays and lighters.

- Your iPod Shuffle held 120 songs.

- You had 12 magazine subscriptions.

- You dropped your film off at a FOTOMAT in a Woolco parking lot.

- Danielle Steel and Stephen King had only written 50 books combined.

- You had a MySpace account.

- Zombies were a musical group.

- "Sustainable" meant making it through an 8-hour shift on the tradeshow floor after partying until 5 am.

- Mr. Coffee was all the coffee you ever needed.

What did we miss? We'd love to hear your clues.

What's So Funny About Trade Shows?

www.ingramcontent.com/pod-product-compliance
Lightning Source LLC
Chambersburg PA
CBHW051216220526
45473CB00003B/1056